# JACKRABBIT VS. SIDEWINDER

BY NATHAN SOMMER

BELLWETHER MEDIA • MINNEAPOLIS, MN

Torque brims with excitement
perfect for thrill-seekers of all kinds.
Discover daring survival skills, explore
uncharted worlds, and marvel at mighty
engines and extreme sports. In *Torque* books,
anything can happen. Are you ready?

This edition first published in 2025 by Bellwether Media, Inc.

No part of this publication may be reproduced in whole or in part without
written permission of the publisher.
For information regarding permission, write to Bellwether Media, Inc.,
Attention: Permissions Department,
6012 Blue Circle Drive, Minnetonka, MN 55343.

Library of Congress Cataloging-in-Publication Data

LC record for Jackrabbit vs. Sidewinder available at:
https://lccn.loc.gov/2024019781

Editor: Suzane Nguyen      Designer: Hunter Demmin

Printed in the United States of America, North Mankato, MN.

# TABLE OF CONTENTS

# THE COMPETITORS

The deserts of North America are dangerous homes. But jackrabbits have **adapted**. Their speed and senses help them escape and keep safe from **predators**.

But sidewinders are not easily spotted. These snakes remain hidden and strike **prey** by surprise. Who wins when these creatures face off?

Jackrabbits are large **hares**. They have lean bodies with powerful back legs. The **mammals** are known for their long ears. These grow up to 7 inches (17.8 centimeters) long!

There are six types of jackrabbits. The hares are found throughout central, southern, and western North America. They make homes in grasslands, deserts, and farmland.

BLACK-TAILED JACKRABBIT

## PLANT EATERS

Jackrabbits mostly eat grass, leaves, and twigs.

# BLACK-TAILED JACKRABBIT PROFILE

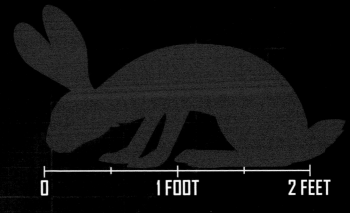

```
0                  1 FOOT              2 FEET
```

**LENGTH**
UP TO 2 FEET
(0.6 METERS)

**WEIGHT**
UP TO 9 POUNDS
(4 KILOGRAMS)

**HABITATS**

GRASSLANDS

DESERTS

FARMLAND

**BLACK-TAILED JACKRABBIT RANGE**

⬛ RANGE

# SIDEWINDER PROFILE

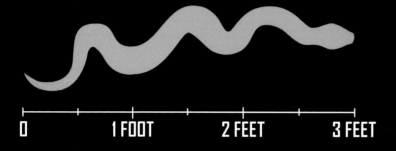

```
├──────┼──────┼──────┼──────┼──────┤
0          1 FOOT        2 FEET        3 FEET
```

**LENGTH**
UP TO 3 FEET
(0.9 METERS)

**WEIGHT**
UP TO 0.7 POUNDS
(0.3 KILOGRAMS)

**HABITAT**

DESERTS

**SIDEWINDER RANGE**

▮ RANGE

Sidewinders are a type of rattlesnake. They have tan scales, white bellies, and small horns above their eyes. The **reptiles** are named for their sideways movements. These help them move quickly across hot sand.

Sidewinders are found in the deserts of southwestern North America. The snakes often find homes in **burrows** made by other animals.

## GROW UP FAST

Sidewinders can live independently within three hours of being born.

# SECRET WEAPONS

Jackrabbits have eyes on the sides of their head. This allows them to see in every direction. The hares easily spot movements from nearby predators.

Sidewinders are the world's fastest snakes. The snakes travel at speeds of up to 18 miles (29 kilometers) per hour. They can move easily across sand to catch prey!

# TOP SPEED

18 MILES (29 KILOMETERS) PER HOUR

**SIDEWINDER**

28 MILES (45 KILOMETERS) PER HOUR

**FASTEST HUMAN**

## LEAPING DISTANCE

**JACKRABBIT**
20 FEET (6.1 METERS)

**LONG JUMP WORLD RECORD**
29.36 FEET (8.95 METERS)

| 0 | 10 FEET | 20 FEET | 30 FEET |

Powerful back legs help jackrabbits escape danger. The hares can run in short bursts of up to 40 miles (64 kilometers) per hour. They can leap up to 20 feet (6.1 meters) when frightened.

Sidewinders have **pit organs** between their eyes and nose. These sense heat given off by nearby prey. The snakes can find their food without even seeing it!

PIT ORGAN

ALL-AROUND VISION    POWERFUL BACK LEGS    CAMOUFLAGE

Jackrabbits easily blend into their **habitats**. Their light brown fur helps them **camouflage** against the desert brush. This makes it hard for predators to spot them.

**SIDEWINDER**

SPEED

PIT ORGANS

FANGS

Sidewinders have curved, razor-sharp **fangs**. They sink these into prey to deliver **venom**. The venom quickly **paralyzes** prey. This makes their meals easy to eat!

# ATTACK MOVES

Jackrabbits use speed to escape danger. They quickly leap and zigzag away from enemies. The hares jump over objects. This causes predators to lose sight of them.

Sidewinders **ambush** their meals. They bury themselves in loose sand. This makes the snakes hard to see. Then, they strike prey that come close!

## A WARNING RATTLE

Sidewinders shake their rattles when scared. The noise warns enemies to stay away.

Jackrabbits fight back when attacked. The hares bite their enemies. They also deliver strong kicks with their back legs to defend themselves.

Sidewinders **lunge** at prey to deliver a deadly bite. Then, the snakes swallow their meals whole. The reptiles often hide underground to **digest** their catch.

# READY, FIGHT!

A hidden sidewinder watches a jackrabbit. The jackrabbit hops near the buried sidewinder. The snake lunges at the jackrabbit. It sinks its fangs into the hare's neck.

The startled jackrabbit fights back with a strong kick. Then, it quickly zigzags away. But soon the jackrabbit slows down. It is defeated by the sidewinder's venom. The sneaky sidewinder wins today!

# GLOSSARY

**adapted**—changed over a long period of time to fit an area

**ambush**—to carry out a surprise attack

**burrows**—tunnels or holes in the ground used as animal homes

**camouflage**—to use colors and patterns to help an animal hide in its surroundings

**digest**—to break down food

**fangs**—long, sharp teeth

**habitats**—the homes or areas where animals prefer to live

**hares**—fast animals that look like rabbits but have larger ears and back legs

**lunge**—to move forward quickly

**mammals**—warm-blooded animals that have backbones and feed their young milk

**paralyzes**—makes unable to move

**pit organs**—special parts that allow snakes to detect the movements of prey in darkness

**predators**—animals that hunt other animals for food

**prey**—animals that are hunted by other animals for food

**reptiles**—cold-blooded animals that have backbones and lay eggs

**venom**—a kind of poison used to hurt or paralyze enemies

# TO LEARN MORE

## AT THE LIBRARY

Boutland, Craig. *Sidewinder*. Minneapolis, Minn.: Bearport Publishing Company, 2021.

Johnson, Rebecca L. *A Walk in the Desert*. Minneapolis, Minn.: Lerner Publications, 2021.

Roggio, Sarah. *Hawks vs. Rattlesnakes: Food Chain Fights*. Minneapolis, Minn.: Lerner Publications, 2025.

## ON THE WEB

# FACTSURFER

Factsurfer.com gives you a safe, fun way to find more information.

1. Go to www.factsurfer.com

2. Enter "jackrabbit vs. sidewinder" into the search box and click 🔍.

3. Select your book cover to see a list of related web sites.

# INDEX

The images in this book are reproduced through the courtesy of: Danita Delimont, front cover (jackrabbit), pp. 4, 18; Chad Lane/ Flickr, front cover (sidewinder) p. 15 (main, fangs); Barnes Ian, pp. 2-3, 20-24; Alizada Studios, pp. 2-3, 20-24; Rusty Dodson, p. 5; Wirestock Creators, pp. 6-7; Mark_Kostich, pp. 8-9, 13; Ingrid Curry, p. 10; MSMondadori, p. 11; Supercaliphotolistic, p. 12; yhelfman, p. 14 (main); ranchorunner, p. 14 (vision); J Curtis, p. 14 (back legs); Jeffrey T. Kreulen, p. 14 (camouflage); Creeping Things, p. 15 (speed); Casey K. Bishop, p. 15 (pit organs); Rob Palmer Photography, p. 16; Vladislav T. Jirousek, p. 17; Rick & Nora Bowers/ Alamy, p. 19.